GOVERNOR MIFFLIN SCHOOL DISTRICT

Presented to:

BRECKNOCK LIBRARY

from: BRECKNOCK PTA
1998 – 1999

Soil

Soil

631.4

Karen Bryant-Mole

Photographs by Barrie Watts

RSVP
RAINTREE
STECK-VAUGHN
PUBLISHERS
The Steck-Vaughn Company

Austin, Texas

Published by Raintree Steck-Vaughn Publishers, an imprint of Steck-Vaughn Company

Editor: Kathy DeVico
Project Manager: Lyda Guz
Electronic Production: Scott Melcer

All photographs by Barrie Watts except: p. 15 David Woodfall/NHPA; p. 24 John Wilkinson/Ecoscene.

Library of Congress Cataloging-in-Publication Data
Bryant-Mole, Karen.
    Soil / Karen Bryant-Mole; photographs by Barrie Watts.
       p.   cm. — (See for yourself)
    Includes index.
    ISBN 0-8172-4213-9
    1. Soils—Juvenile literature.   2. Soil biology—Juvenile literature. [1. Soils. 2. Soil biology.] I. Watts, Barrie, ill.
II. Title. III. Series.
S591.3.B65   1996
631.4—dc20
                                  95-33271
                                        CIP
                                        AC

Printed and bound in the United States
1 2 3 4 5 6 7 8 9 0 99 98 97 96 95

Contents

Layers of Soil

Can you think of some places where you might find soil? In gardens? Or in fields, perhaps? Both answers are right. But soil is found in many other places, too.

Soil covers our planet, Earth.
Look at the big picture. Can you see the different layers in the soil? The topsoil is dark brown. Underneath the topsoil there is another layer, called subsoil.

Deep down, underneath the subsoil, there is rock.

The girl in this picture has found soil around the bottom of a tree. Where else might you find soil?

What Is Soil Made Of?

Soil is made up of a mixture of things.
Most of it comes from pieces of rock.

The pieces of rock come in lots of different
sizes. The biggest pieces are stones.
Stony soil can be very difficult to dig into.

Smaller pieces of rock have different names.
They are called gravel, sand, silt, or clay.

To find out what soil is
made of, put some into
a jar of water. Shake the
mixture up, and then
leave it to settle.

In a few days, you should
find that the soil has
settled into layers.
The gravel will be at the
bottom, then the sand,
and silt. The clay will
be on the top.

Humus

In the soil, there are millions of tiny living things, such as fungi and bacteria. Fungi and bacteria feed on bits of dead plants and animals that fall onto the soil. They help the dead plants and animals to rot into a dark, sticky substance, called humus.

You can see the white threads of fungi in the big picture. The photograph was taken through a microscope. Microscopes make things look much bigger than they really are.

You can see how plants rot by making a compost pile. Make layers of garden clippings, fruit and vegetable peelings, and soil. This girl has made her compost pile in a plastic box.

Leave it alone for a month or so. What changes do you notice?

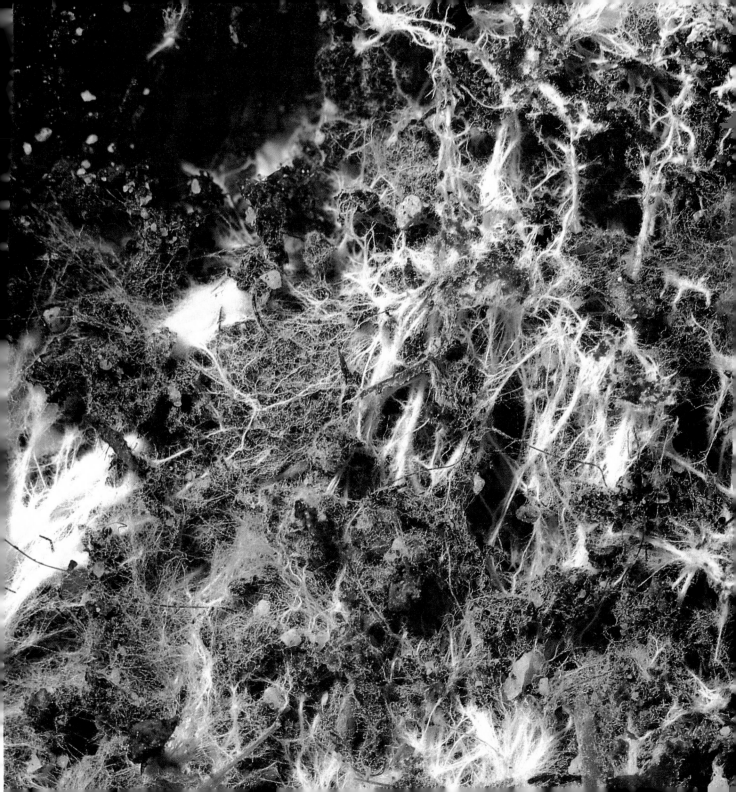

Why Plants Need Soil

Most plants send roots out into the soil. Their roots
suck up water from the soil. This water is full of good
things from the humus and from the tiny bits of rock.
It is like liquid food for the plants. It helps them to grow.

Soil is often covered by plants. Even bare soil usually
has tiny plant seeds in it, just waiting to sprout.

Fill a large pot with soil.
Water it, and keep it warm.

Small plants will soon
start to grow in the soil.

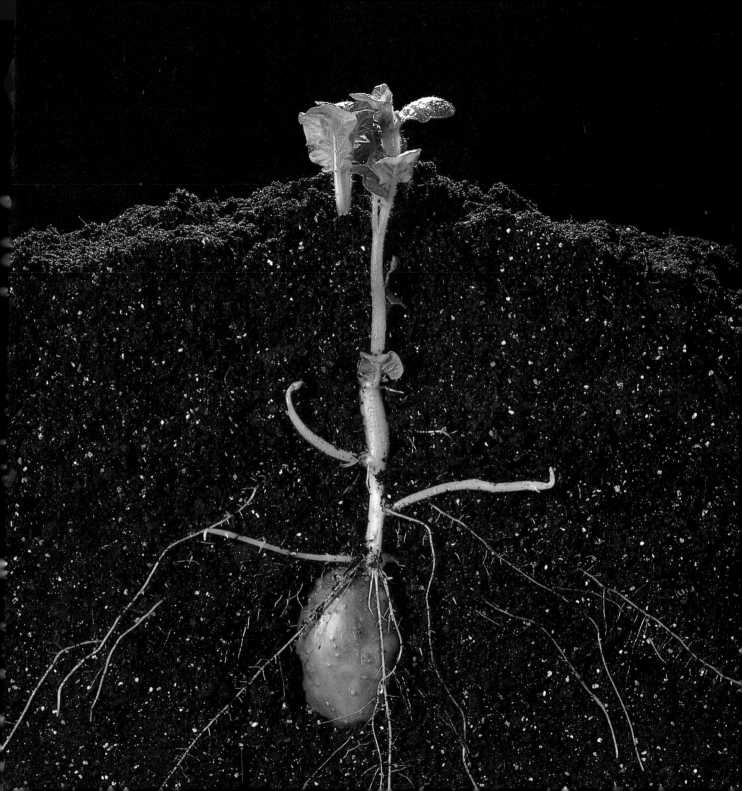

Keeping Soil Fertile

Gardeners and farmers grow crops, flowers, and vegetables. As these plants grow, they use up the goodness, or nutrients, in the soil.

If farmers and gardeners want to keep growing strong plants, they have to find a way of putting the goodness back into the soil. This is called fertilizing the soil.

The farmers in the big picture are spreading chemical fertilizer onto the field. This is an easy way to make the soil good for growing crops.

Many gardeners prefer to use a more natural fertilizer, however. This man is shoveling some horse manure into his garden. Shoveling in manure or compost adds extra humus to the soil.

How Earthworms Help Soil

As earthworms wiggle along underground, they dig and mix the soil. Their tunnels keep the soil airy and make passages for rainwater to run through.

Earthworms pull dead leaves down into the soil and eat them. The leaves pass through the earthworms. Once they come out of the earthworms, it is easier for the fungi and bacteria to work on them. So, earthworms help leaves to rot more quickly.

You can see some of these things by making a wormery. Ask an adult to cut the top off a plastic bottle. Fill the bottle with layers of soil and sand. Put some dead leaves on the top, and keep the wormery dark. Keep the soil mix moist.

Add two earthworms. What do you notice?

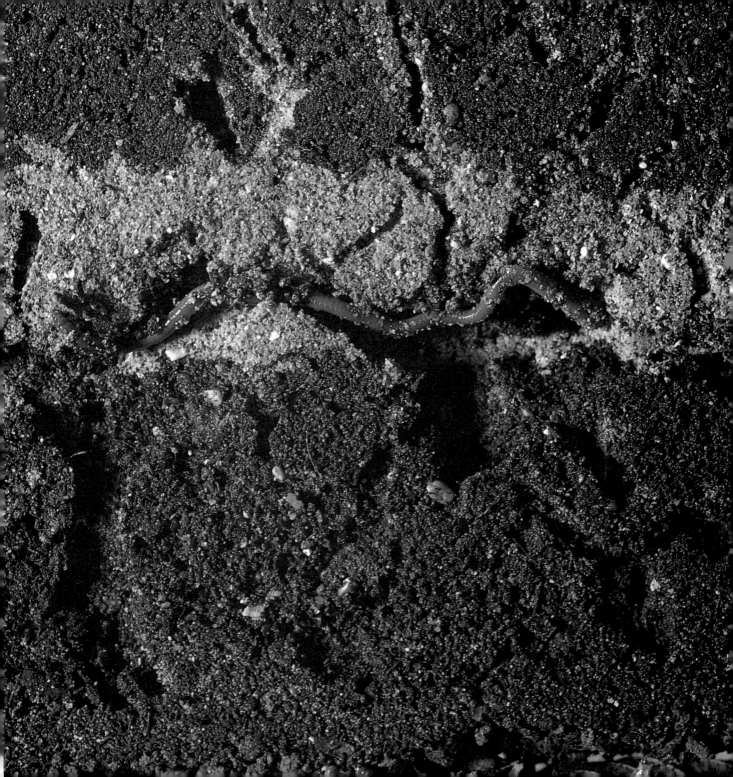

Insect Life

Lots of small insects, like the wood lice in the big picture, live in or on soil. Wood lice feed on dead wood and leaves that have fallen onto the soil. This helps to turn the wood and leaves into humus.

You can usually find wood lice, beetles, or earwigs under stones or rotten logs.

Some insects live underground. Ants, wireworms, and springtails all live in the soil.

You could look for some tiny insects yourself. Put a soil sample into a funnel. Put the funnel into a tall jar. Place a light over the funnel. The insects in the soil will dig downward to get away from the light. They will fall into the jar.

Put the soil sample and insects back where you found them.

Animal Homes

Many of the animals that live in soil are very small.
However, some, like the mole in the big picture,
are much larger.

Moles dig long tunnels under fields and gardens.
They use their strong front paws to dig. They push the
soil from their tunnels up to the surface into small piles.
These piles of earth are called molehills. Moles scurry
through their tunnels, looking for small insects to eat.

Foxes, badgers, and
rabbits all make tunnels
through soil, too.
Their homes have special
names. This badger lives
in a home called a set.

Can you find out the
name of a fox's home
and the name for
a rabbit's home?

Types of Soil

Chalky soil contains pieces of chalk rock. Sandy soil has lots of sand in it. Clay soil is made up of very tiny pieces of different rocks. Loams are a mixture of clay soil and sandy soil.

Rainwater soaks through sandy and chalky soils very easily. Clay soils stay wet and sticky for a while, after it has rained. Loams can hold some rainwater without becoming sticky. Soils that are sold at garden centers are usually loams.

You can test your own soil. Put pieces of gauze inside two funnels. Place the funnels inside some tall jelly jars. Put some local soil in one jar and some garden center soil in the other. Pour the same amount of water into both.

Soil that holds more water than the garden center soil is probably clay. Soil that holds less water is probably sandy or chalky.

clay soil

sandy soil

chalky soil

Saving Soil

A strong wind can blow soil away. Usually trees, hedges, and other plants keep this from happening. Also, the tangle of roots in the soil keeps the soil from being washed away by rain.

But in some places around the world, whole forests of trees have been cut down. Look at the big picture. Can you see where the trees have been cut down? Without plants, the soil can be blown or washed away.

Much of the wood from the forests is used to make paper and cardboard. Most of this only gets used once and is then thrown away.

This truck is taking old paper to a recycling center, where the paper is made ready to be used again.

Recycling paper means that fewer trees need to be cut down, and thus less soil is lost.

Soil Feeds the World

There are millions of people in the world,
and they all need food.

The big picture shows a field of barley. Barley can
be used to make breads and breakfast cereals.

Fruits, vegetables, and grains all come from
plants that grow in soil.

We would not have meat, eggs, milk, or cheese
if it were not for soil. Can you figure out why?
The girl in this picture is giving you a hint!

Cows eat grass, which grows
in soil. The cows produce
milk, which we can drink.
Can you find out how soil
helps us to have eggs?
Draw a picture about it.

Think about all the food that
we eat. You will find that soil
really does feed the world.

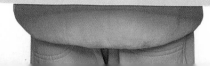

More Things to Do

1. Make a model.
Modeling clay is very similar to clay soil. When it is wet, it is heavy and sticky. You can mold modeling clay into all sorts of shapes. When it dries out, it becomes very hard.

2. Tasty tomatoes
Why not use soil to grow something that you can eat? Homegrown tomatoes taste delicious. You can grow them from seeds, or you can buy small tomato plants.

3. Rain dancing
Worms come up to the surface of the soil when it rains. Try jumping up and down on the ground. Sometimes this tricks the worms into thinking it is raining, and they will come up out of the ground!

4. Will it rot?
Some things rot more quickly than others, and some things don't rot at all. Dig four holes in some soil. Put a piece of apple peel in one, a scrap of newspaper in another, a piece of cabbage leaf in the third, and a little piece from a plastic bag in the fourth. Label each one with a marker. One month later, dig up all four things. Which has rotted the most? Which has rotted the least?

Index

This index will help you find some
of the important words in this book.

Notes for Parents and Teachers

These notes will give you some additional information about soil and suggest some more activities you might like to try with children.

Pages 6–7
Soil is arranged in layers that are sometimes known as horizons. Underneath a thin, top layer, there is the dark, humus-rich topsoil. Below this is the subsoil, which contains less humus but is full of minerals that have been washed down from the topsoil. The next layer consists mainly of pieces of rock, and the layer below that is solid rock.

Pages 8–9
In this activity, you will find that the soil settles in layers according to the size of the rock pieces. The largest (and heaviest) pieces of rock, the gravel, will be at the bottom, and the finest pieces, the clay, will be at the top. There may be organic matter floating on the water.

Pages 10–11
Rotting is the process by which living organisms, such as bacteria and fungi, work on dead plant and animal matter and break it down into chemical salts, such as nitrates and phosphates. These chemical salts are food for plants and help them to grow new shoots, leaves, and roots. Some animals, such as earthworms, also assist the rotting process by eating and excreting organic material. Inorganic materials, such as plastics, cannot rot. Children should be encouraged to think about the consequences of inorganic litter.

Pages 14–15
Chemical fertilizers are used by many farmers as a fast and cheap way of improving the soil. Children could investigate the pros and cons of chemical fertilizers. Other methods of keeping the soil fertile could be examined, such as the use of crop rotation, which works on the principle that some plants deplete the soil of certain minerals, while other plants restore them.

Pages 24–25
Soil erosion is a big problem in some parts of the world, such as Central and South America. In addition to deforestation, other causes of soil erosion include the overfarming of land and the removal of hedges to create larger fields. Hedges act as windbreaks. Without them, the wind can sweep across fields, removing soil from the surface.

Pages 26–27
These pages are an introduction to the idea of food chains. An example of a food chain is this: a fox, which eats a bird, which eats a caterpillar, which eats leaves. All food chains eventually lead back to plant life. If something happens to one element of the food chain, it can affect the other elements of the chain. For instance, when the insecticide DDT was used on plants, it not only killed insects, but those insects poisoned animals farther up the food chain. Often, food chains are linked. Humans eat rabbits, and so do foxes. These linked food chains all form a food web.